Showdown

Alpha Animals

Saskia Lacey

Publishing Credits

Rachelle Cracchiolo, M.S.Ed., *Publisher*
Conni Medina, M.A.Ed., *Managing Editor*
Nika Fabienke, Ed.D., *Series Developer*
June Kikuchi, *Content Director*
John Leach, *Assistant Editor*
Lee Aucoin, *Senior Graphic Designer*

Library of Congress Cataloging-in-Publication Data

Names: Lacey, Saskia, author.
Title: Showdown : alpha animals / Saskia Lacey.
Description: Huntington Beach, CA : Teacher Created Materials, [2018] | Audience: Grade K to Grade 3. | Includes index.
Identifiers: LCCN 2017013466 (print) | LCCN 2017014386 (ebook) | ISBN 9781425853501 (eBook) | ISBN 9781425849764 (pbk.)
Subjects: LCSH: Social hierarchy in animals—Juvenile literature. | Social behavior in animals—Juvenile literature.
Classification: LCC QL775 (ebook) | LCC QL775 .L23 2018 (print) | DDC 591.56—dc23
LC record available at https://lccn.loc.gov/2017013466

Teacher Created Materials
5301 Oceanus Drive
Huntington Beach, CA 92649-1030
http://www.tcmpub.com
ISBN 978-1-4258-4976-4
© 2018 Teacher Created Materials, Inc.

Index

Check It Out!

Books

Claybourne, Anna. 2012. *A Pack of Wolves: and Other Canine Groups*. Heinemann.

Goodall, Jane. 1996. *My Life with the Chimpanzees*. Aladdin.

Videos

National Geographic. "Big Ram Rumble." YouTube.

National Geographic. "A Silverback Showdown." National Geographic Channel.

National Geographic. "Wolf Hunting Tactics." YouTube.

Websites

National Geographic. *Animals*. www.nationalgeographic.com/animals/.

Smithsonian's National Zoo & Conservation Biology Institute. nationalzoo.si.edu/animals.

Try It!

You might have heard of a family tree, but what about a wolf family tree? Most wolf packs are family groups. Create a chart of an imaginary wolf family. Show the connections between the different members of the pack.

- 🐾 How many wolves are in the pack? How are they related?

- 🐾 Who is the alpha? What is this wolf's role in the pack?

- 🐾 What are the roles of the other wolves?

- 🐾 Are there any rivalries in the pack?

- 🐾 Write a story about your wolf pack forming.

About the Author

Saskia Lacey is the author of *Jurassic Classics: The Prehistoric Masters of Literature* and *Technical Tales: How to Build a Plane*, as well as 15 other books. Someday, she hopes to write a book about the pack behavior of domestic dogs. Her favorite pack animal is her dog, Lily, who is the alpha in her house!

Table of Contents

Pack Animals: Better Together?

Surviving in the wild isn't easy. There are **predators** around every corner. You must be able to rely on your **pack**. Out here, it's eat or be eaten. There is no in-between. Some animals are alphas, the leaders of packs. Other animals are followers. They support the alphas.

There is conflict in every animal **community**. But some groups have more than others. The fierce mountain gorilla will fight to protect his group. The alpha wolf will bite and scratch to stay at the head of his pack. Each of these **species** battles for power. They have to. The lives of their packs depend on them!

Fierce and Furry

During breeding season, male brown fur seals battle for **territory**. Growling and honking, they charge each other. These beasts are willing to fight to the death.

Locking Horns

Bighorn rams are famous for their head-butting contests. They lock their 40-pound (18-kilogram) horns with each other. These fights determine each ram's place in the herd. Luckily, these animals have double-layered skulls to protect them.

Jungle Jousts

Western lowland gorillas are unique. They are very **social**. They live in groups called troops. During their lives, they may move a few times. As a result, these gorillas must be able to **adapt**.

The group that a gorilla is born into is called its **natal** (NAY-tuhl) troop. Once gorillas are old enough, they can leave their homes. Or they might stay with their natal troops.

Save the Gorillas

Western lowland gorillas are critically endangered. Their numbers have declined in recent years. This means that these gorillas might become **extinct**.

The Nose Knows

Humans have unique patterns on
their fingers. No two people have
the same fingerprint. Gorillas have
patterns on their fingers, too. But
they also have unique noseprints.
This means no nose is the same!

Growing Up Gorilla

As babies, mountain gorillas depend on their mothers. They always stay close to their mothers. Baby gorillas eat, sleep, and travel with their mothers. Some ride on their mothers' backs until they are two or three years old.

As gorillas grow up, they have to make a choice. Should they stay with their troops? Or should they leave? Some males choose to stay with their natal troops. They might replace the alpha males of their troops when the time comes.

Alpha Females

Bonobos aren't like other apes. Alpha females lead their troops. Young females move to new groups. Males stay in their natal troops, close to their mothers.

Other male gorillas choose to leave their natal troops. Some join other groups with males and females. Some join troops made up of only young male gorillas. These are called bachelor troops.

Sometimes, a gorilla will try to form his own troop. This can be dangerous. The gorilla may have to steal female gorillas from another troop. This means he will have to challenge the alpha!

A Jungle Roar

When gorillas battle, it is loud. They grunt, growl, bark, and roar. They beat their chests. Battles can happen within a troop. Battles can also happen outside of a troop.

Top Boss

In a gorilla troop, the alpha is the most powerful. He controls when the troop eats, sleeps, and travels. What the alpha says, goes!

From Troop to Troop

Female gorillas move from troop to troop, too. Once a female is mature, she can stay with her natal group. Or she might join another.

Females choose a new home by studying the troop's alpha. They want to know that they will have a place in the new group. They also want to be in a group that has a strong leader. Females choose the alphas with a lot of territory. They might join several troops during their lives.

The Bigger, the Better

Battles are not always violent between gorillas. Sometimes, they will charge at each other but won't touch. Alphas can earn the top spots in troops just by being the biggest.

Dog-Eat-Dog World

Gray wolves are the largest **canine** species. They are also known as timber wolves. These fierce creatures are pack animals that travel, eat, sleep, and hunt together.

Packs usually have six to eight wolves, but some packs are much bigger. They can have up to two dozen wolves. Most packs are families. The members of the pack are the **offspring** of the alpha male and alpha female. These two wolves are the **dominant** members of the pack. They guide all pack behavior.

Protect the Pups

Pups, or baby wolves, are treasured by the entire wolf pack. They are looked after by all the wolves in their group. When they are very young, they are protected in dens.

Speaking Wolf

When wolves talk to each other, they howl, yelp, and whine. The sound of a wolf's howl can be heard for miles. A howl can mean many different things. Wolves howl to keep track of each other and to let the pack know when they have found food.

Wolves also communicate with their bodies. When a wolf challenges another wolf, it will raise its **hackles** and growl. Alpha wolves also use this behavior to show their **rank** in the pack. **Submissive** wolves show their rank by lying on the ground and pawing at the alphas.

Telling Tails

You can tell a lot about a canine by its tail. When a wolf is approaching a dominant member of its pack, its tail and body stay low. However, a dominant wolf walks tall and keeps its tail high.

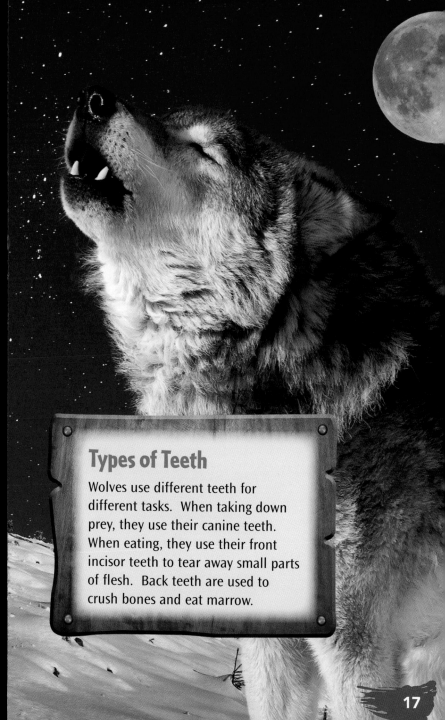

Types of Teeth

Wolves use different teeth for different tasks. When taking down prey, they use their canine teeth. When eating, they use their front incisor teeth to tear away small parts of flesh. Back teeth are used to crush bones and eat marrow.

Mealtime Manners

While it may not appear so from the outside, wolves follow rules during meals. Once prey has been caught, wolves dine in a certain order. The alpha pair gets the first choice. Once they have eaten, lower-ranking wolves will have a chance to feed. Once the rest of the pack has eaten, the lowest members take their turn. These wolves are usually the youngest of the pack.

Wolves don't always succeed at catching their prey. Sometimes they go more than a week without eating. Wolves can eat as much as 20 pounds (9 kilograms) of meat at once to make up for periods without food. After that, they can rest for a few days before hunting again.

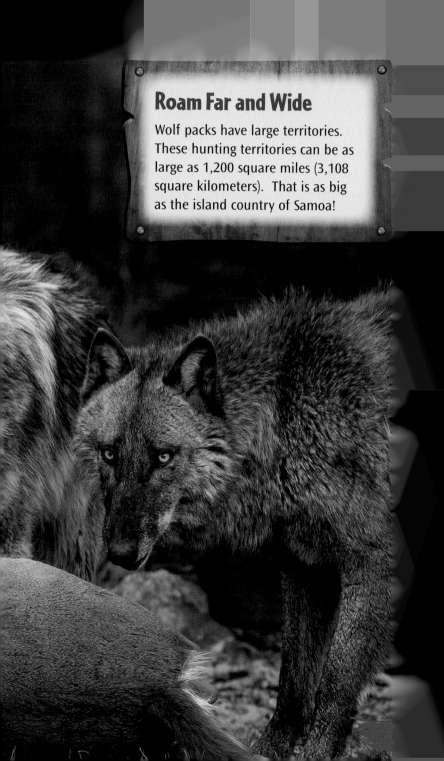

Roam Far and Wide

Wolf packs have large territories. These hunting territories can be as large as 1,200 square miles (3,108 square kilometers). That is as big as the island country of Samoa!

Run of the Roost

It might not look like it, but chickens can be tough. These birds aren't afraid to fight for what they want. Chickens peck each other to set their rank in the flock. Sometimes, this pecking can turn deadly.

Usually, rank is set quickly. If there is a rooster in the flock, he becomes the alpha. If the flock has two roosters, they will compete for the top spot. If there are no roosters, one hen will peck her way to the alpha position. Stronger and healthier chickens are ranked higher than weak and sickly birds.

Best Feather Friends

Hens have friends, just like people. They stay close to each other during the day. According to some chicken owners, if a hen's best friend leaves, the hen will stay where she last saw her friend.

Rooster vs. Human

Roosters and hens see humans as
their alphas. Well, they usually
do. Sometimes, roosters try to
dominate humans. Watch out for
that beak!

Pecking and Squawking

Problems arise when new chickens are introduced to a flock. Pecking starts again, and all chickens must fight to keep their rank.

Sometimes, chickens will gang up on one hen and peck her repeatedly. This hen must be taken away from the group in order to survive. Otherwise, the flock might peck her to death. If a hen is killed, the other chickens might eat her.

Chickens are **vocal**. They cluck and squawk to communicate. The alpha rooster or hen calls to let the flock know about food or danger. Alphas have an important role. They look out for the rest of the flock.

Proud Mamas

When hens lay eggs, they announce it with clucks and calls. They want the world to know. This is another example of how chickens communicate.

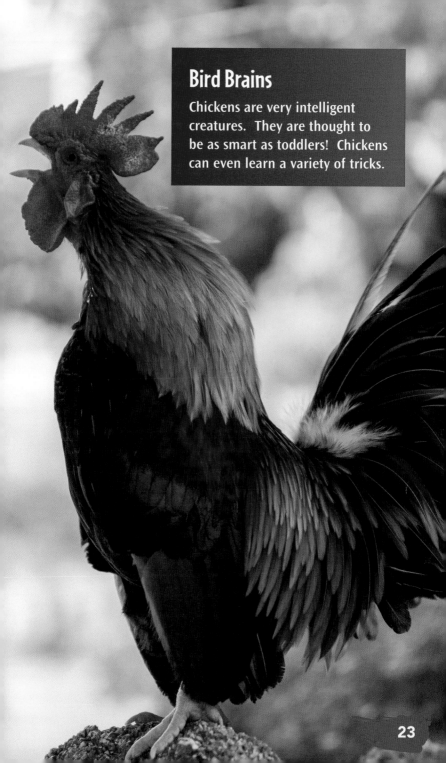

Bird Brains

Chickens are very intelligent creatures. They are thought to be as smart as toddlers! Chickens can even learn a variety of tricks.

Hen House

Chickens need room to move around and flap their wings. Often, chickens are kept in small spaces. These spaces can become overcrowded. As a result, the chickens might become more violent.

Pecking happens more often in small spaces. In part, this is because there is less bonding between chickens. It is hard to create a bond with hundreds of other chickens around.

Animals need space to live and grow. This space should be clean and comfortable. There are many farms that have free-range chickens. This means that chickens are able to roam outside. They can exercise and explore!

Egg-Laying Machines

Hens can start laying eggs when they are around six months old. Hens lay eggs during the summer in the wild. On farms, chickens lay eggs year-round. One hen can lay as many as 300 eggs in a year!

Free-Range Chickens

Responsible farms provide lots of space for chickens to roam. Free-range chickens spend their lives outside. They have room to perch, fly, and take dust baths!

Stronger Together

Being a part of an animal group is not easy. Whether it is a troop, pack, or flock, the struggle to survive is real. Each member of the group has duties. Alphas must prove their strength and protect their groups. The rest must follow the alpha's lead or risk a fight.

Animal groups provide safety. There is a better chance of survival when animals are together. They look out for one another. When danger is close, they warn one another. When food is found, they celebrate together. It is a struggle, but it is worth it!

Bold Bubbles

Some dolphins show aggression in unique ways. They chase one another and slap their tails on the water. They also blow bubbles from their blowholes!

King of the Kangaroos

In kangaroo groups, usually one
male becomes the alpha. He is the
biggest and strongest of the bunch.
He bites, kicks, and boxes his rivals.

Glossary

adapt—to change to make life easier

canine—a dog or an animal related to a dog

community—a group that lives in the same area

dominant—more important, powerful, or successful than most or all others

extinct—no longer existing

hackles—hairs on the back of a wolf's neck

natal—related to one's birth

offspring—the young of a person, animal, or plant

pack—a group of animals that live and hunt together

predators—animals that live by killing and eating other animals

rank—position in a society, organization, or group

social—tending to form relationships and live together in groups

species—things of the same kind and with the same name

submissive—allowing others to be in charge

territory—an area that an animal or group uses and defends

vocal—making loud noise